How to Rise Above Your Emotions

By Emotional Literacy Specialist
Cassandra Lea Wilson B.A., RYT

ISBN #978-1-988949-10-9

This work is dedicated to all of the people who need help with their emotions, to understand them, to sort them, to process and allow them so that they can experience them as the true gift they are.

And also to my family, who enabled me to see emotions as a tool.

Introduction

The biggest question we humans seem to have about emotions is, How can we not have emotions?

In researching our biggest question about emotions for this ebook, I found that the most common question is some form of How can I change, manipulate or 'kill' my emotions so they are no longer in my life?

Other poignant questions I found online were:
How do I control my emotions?
How can I use my emotions constructively?
Why do other people ignore or invalidate my emotions?
How can I hide my emotions?
How can I understand and 'deal with' myself?
Will I outgrow my emotions as I get older?
How can I save my emotions for later?
How do I understand and work with other people's emotions?
How can I switch my emotions on and off?

As you can see from this cursory research I conducted, I was easily uncovering questions with one thing in common. What are emotions good for anyway?

Despite the resounding Nothing that seems to emanate from these questions, I'm here to debunk that assertion.

The Transformation

I am the anomaly when it comes to this subject. I love emotions. And I'll tell you why.

I grew up in a typical household in the seventies and eighties. My parents were the typical parents at that time and there were no discussions about emotions or the handling of them. There were only outbursts, then calms. This wavy environment in which I lived, made me think that emotions were a tornado you did well to stay out of. I witnessed these tornadoes from time to time until I found myself in the eye of my own tornadoes as I aged. 'There was nothing wrong with me. It was them, or her, or him who needed to change.'

Taking this external orientation into my twenties, I was challenged by various situations, feeling the lash of the winds in circumstances here and there until I found myself on a beach in Thailand.

Just as if I had been flung out of the tornado like a pebble, I found the most tranquil, serene beach I had ever witnessed. This beach seemed like it was from another world. It was so still. The sand was as soft as powder. The palm trees arched lazily and comfortably beside the azure water. The bubble and swish of the gentle waves upon the shore had a mesmerizing effect upon my consciousness. And as days went by, I became still as well. But that which was inside me that was not still, began to emerge within me.

That's right. My emotions.

They began to rise to the surface, calling me back to the moment of their inception. I began to roll back and forth, clutching my stomach in pain as I energetically birthed, or purged, the sorrows I had been carrying - the judgment, the sadness, the feelings of being misunderstood. And as each messy ball of emotion came to the surface of my consciousness, I witnessed my life open up as each emotion finally popped in a culmination of release to the wisdom held within.

It was breathtaking. I was stunned. Underneath the rubble of pain and sadness and inner toil, there was a light at the end of the tunnel, a butterfly of truth revealing itself to my consciousness.

My mother does love me.

It wasn't about me.

It wasn't my fault.

I'm okay.

The truths fell into my lap, shifting my perspective from years of worry and sadness and self doubt about who I was and what my purpose was. My soul began to awaken beneath the surface of this weightiness and emerge as a powerful bright guiding light beaming through the surface of my mundane and previously dim perspective.

Resolution became my friend. And the true beauty of resolution is that No one was to blame. Everyone emerged from my feeling vortex as innocent. I didn't have to make wrong anyone! No one was the perpetrator! We had all danced so that we could all have the opportunity to reach deeper into ourselves where the real truth resided.

Once I began this journey of allowing my emotions to have their say, I started to feel better. Sometimes, even often, I cried as I allowed their truths to come forth. But each and every time they brought gifts of new awareness that rose above my previous notions on the subject. It was a discovery of dusting off the best possible point of view! I was emerging from my own depths of blame, sorrow and inner pain.

I began to let my emotions take the helm. I sat ready and waiting for a new bubble to emerge, a new contraction of feeling which connected me more deeply to myself and purged itself of the untruth that had laid within me, covered with the dust and grime of judgement and incomplete thought.

Incomplete Thought

The habit we have of thinking about something until something else swoops into our minds is rampant in our western society. There are so many things happening at once that we are easily distracted. So when something happens in our lives that cause us to feel emotion, we often don't give the feeling and situation enough time in our consciousness to come to a clear resolution. We often blame the other person, or ourselves and consider the matter dealt with. But this practice loads our psyche with unfinished business and clutters our emotional 'inbox'. And until we take the time to sort through this inbox, we carry those burdens of blame and anger around in our energy fields, and they inadvertently dim our perspective of life and cause us to grow in cynicism, bitterness and un-forgiveness. I had to learn the practice of allowing situations that had not yet been resolved and cleared in my memory, the ample room to expand until each bubble popped with new awareness. At the bottom of every nuance is the pure truth that we love each other dearly. Miscommunication is often the culprit for broken relationships. Blame holds the fore for many of us, and it's what we are taught in society.

But these practices of semi-conscious management of our feelings needs to end. Too many of us are on anti-depressants and disenchanted with life. It's my firm belief that a clearing and organizing of unresolved circumstances will allow us the freedom to expand

beyond the confines of anger and the walls of
sadness.

So how do we complete a thought? Think about a
situation that sits inside of you, festering with the
energy of unresolved emotion. It's where blame,
separation and anxiety live when you think about a
person or situation. It's a prime learning ground. It's
where the treasure is buried.

Let yourself wade into the energy. At first you'll find
the 'surface bubbles,' the blaming thoughts, and
disillusion of the messages that rest upon the truth.
These messages will be your own created thoughts
about the situation. Wade in further. You'll find the
flat line of emotion, the pain that you harbour
underneath all of the writhing, unrestful thoughts.
The anger, pain, sadness or betrayal you felt. Feel it
for yourself to understand how you held the energy
and categorized it in your lower consciousness. Often
in this place, we are the victims.

Keep going. You may see visions or images or feel
sensations. You may sense a cloud of white energy, as
white energy indicates trauma. There may have been
a past situation, don't rule out past lives, where the
inciting event is still holding on for processing. We
don't need to know right now. Just witness the place
that holds on.

Stay in the emotion. Your mind will show you images
and you may feel tempted to wander into the story.
Stay in the emotion and follow it down into yourself.

Allow the story to reveal itself from inside the emotion. Feel the sensations, let the memory guide you through. When you can see in your mind's eye what appears to be the inciting event, which may be completely different than the one you originally accessed, allow it to emerge. Witness what that holds.

Perhaps it was a death, betrayal, abandonment, as these themes are pervasive in our psyches. Allow the culmination of the story. Sense the ending. Breathe and allow it to complete in the last scene.

Then once it has completed, add your own new ending. Bring the person back to you in a happy state. See the deceased person as if they had lived, as if they had returned to a happy reunion and your warm embrace. Visualize them reemerging as you had hoped they had and bring about your own happy ending in your mind's eye.

Bring the person into your loving embrace, hold them with love and forgiveness. Allow them to enter through your heart's doorway and into the golden light that heals and transmutes the occurrence. Allow the new ending to rewrite the failed attempt to culminate in a balancing of energy. Now, you can sigh relief.

You released the energy in tears or exhales. You allowed the story to reveal itself. You completed it with a happy ending. That is the work. Now the story has raised itself to a higher vibrational level. It will uplift you and make you feel lighter.

The other stories that await this transmutation will be elevated and await the specific transformation to a place within your psyche where All Is Well.

The completing statement is All Is Well. We know that with God All Is Well. So when we arrive to this knowing, on this topic, we are complete. Well done. This segment of your history has been adjusted in your favour and you will feel better, lighter and happier. Continue to work through your judgments and incomplete thoughts in this same way. Bring them into balance and completion where we are all well.

If you hit a snag and cannot complete in this way, continue your work. If you have to leave the clearing unexpectedly put blue light around it in your mind's eye and say to it, 'I'll be back later. Please let me know when I can come back to complete this'. And soon you will have another chance.

Complete the thoughts. Work to clear your inbox. It can be done. And each time, you clear your psyche and perspective by one degree. Well done.

Hitting A Snag

Here is a list of possible hurdles you will have to overcome if they arise for you. Be patient with yourself, but be aware of these possible derailments and do your best to continue even when you are faced with them.

1. Too much emotion - You may feel a surge of emotion and be uncomfortable or unfamiliar with it. Allow it. Breath and use your breath to usher the wave through its flow and ebb, because it will ebb. Make it easier to experience by going into it, allowing it and letting it out. Cry your eyes out on your bed, sob in release. If you're frightened, think of it as stopping a sneeze. You can stop a sneeze or an emotional wave. But they say it's best to let the bodily processes run their course. It's the same with emotional release. If you feel challenged, 1) Take a bath, 2) Go into nature, 3) Hold a crystal (which always helps transmute emotional energy) or a teddy bear for comfort (this works!) 4) Hold your own shoulders and give yourself a hug.

2. You're interrupted - Put a blue light around the energy, the work, until later. The emotional energy may recede properly, for hours or days, but it will find a good time to emerge when you can process it completely.

3. You feel confused or lost in the process - Sink into the *feeling*. You may be thinking instead of

feeling. Keep going, use the breath to feel the emotion. Stay with the *feeling*. It will make sense at the end of the release.

4. Doubt - 'Is this really true? Are these memories/visions true or just my imagination?' It's all true and has value when you're in the feeling. If your mind is reeling and you're in a thinking mode, it may get messy. Emotional release has one channel and one path. These feelings are deep and outside of the thought realm. They are in a different faculty and you will resonate with the pictures in your mind as if they are familiar in some way. You've lived thousands of lives. This is your story. Anything is possible. Resist the urge to judge and remain as witness.

5. Holding it in or blocking access. The energy isn't moving and you feel stuck. Breathe. Let the air fill your lungs and focus on the movement of your breath until the flow begins again. Set your intention to go within for discovery of stuck energy or repressed emotions in a kind and gentle manner for your highest good. Try not to categorize the story as it unfolds, just feel the message. You can make sense of it intellectually after the emotional release is complete. Do not allow discomfort to hold you back. Growth requires it!

Setting Up The Sanctuary

As you've read, this work can be intense, and so rewarding! Just as archeologists have to travel to distant places and dig in the dirt to discover priceless treasures, this is the same for you. Make a special place for this sacred work and enjoy setting up your sanctuary.

1. Quiet and undisturbed place and time. Hang a sign on the door, lock it, close the blinds if necessary. A little darkness can relax the mind and help you as light takes you to surface consciousness. We are going deeper. Early in the morning or late at night is best when things are calm in your environment. Unless you live in the forest then anytime should work. But again, as you are going deeper, having a less stimulating environment will help your concentration.

2. Light a candle. This is my go to ritual when any emotion emerges or when I'm in meditation and accessing my deeper levels. It's a signal to the spiritual realm that I am entering the 'work space' and may need guidance and support. Of course, I have already established this association. You can call in this connection by saying, 'As I light this candle I am signalling my spiritual helpers to enter and be present to guide and assist me. With thanks and love.' The lighting of this candle creates a special bridge into your heart of awareness and sets a lovely tone for your inner work.

3. Make yourself comfortable on a soft chair with a soft blanket on your lap. This is a period of nurturing. Have a cup of tea or drink beside you. Have a tissue box at hand! Tears are energy releasing and are a sign of forward progress. They cleanse the soul and bring relief. Allow them!

4. Have comforts nearby, signs, symbols and things you love such as pets, soft pillows, etc. This is a sweet sanctuary where you feel safe to open the treasure box within and unpack it.

5. A Journal - Once you have completed a shift in awareness and you feel better, or hear the word complete in your inner thoughts, write down what you learned about yourself and your story. You may want to write a letter to someone if you feel called to do so. You don't have to send it, but this helps a sense of completion. Also, you could write down impressions you received and shifts that took place. Or you may just want to go on with your day, and that's fine, too.

6. Make this practice regular. Just like mowing the lawn, you have to keep at it for the beauty of the grass to present itself. Your cleansing rituals don't have to be on a schedule. When your emotions are ready, you will feel the nudge to access them. Don't put this off if you can do the work. It's best to face the emotion wanting to work its' way out of your energy field. Three weeks would be the maximum time I would wait, unless I wanted to experience and witness them coming out in an

unscheduled outburst. You could start a new ritual at bedtime to light a candle and sit quietly. Make space to feel your feelings and enter a new relationship with yourself with ever greater love.

Family Agreements

Sometimes in my work, I find a client who has a vast history with a specific family member. Often when emotional situations aren't resolved and have festered over lifetimes they can become very dense and appear very complex to resolve. Sometimes they appear to need a lot of work and you will need to work on these situational relationships to help them heal. As you release some of this hidden energy and emotion the person connected to it also heals and releases the emotional charge. Your personal work will have a positive effect on the overall relationship. Something I have learned about this unique relationship is that often the inciting event that caused an energy charge between the two people is an innocent one.

For example, perhaps you were accidentally dropped as a child in this life and the person came to you with a look of horror on their face which was imprinted into your mind when they come to you. Your mind flips to this byte of info and the emotion associated and expects a worrying situation going forward. Or perhaps your loved one perished in another life right before your eyes. You lamented their passing the whole lifetime, feeling terrible, and created an energy charge around sorrow and grief. Then the next life you entered with that charge active and things began too manifest in a new way that holds true to those feelings or energy and emotion. Often we don't know the why or the root cause of our real feelings because they are buried in the distant past. That's why this work is so valuable because once you expose the root cause to your consciousness, you release the emotional energy and a great healing takes place. Perhaps you cared for a dying relative and the experience was very uncomfortable and you held onto that pain and upset. Your energy is brought through you to a new life with that energy charge intact in new circumstances! The thoughts and emotions form the basis for healing and growth in this life, as you hold the frequency and intense need for the healing of that dynamic. Each soul in your family is with you for a specific reason.

Your souls choose to reunite for healing this time for specific reasons. So if you still hold energy for someone in your family that is not balanced in a healthy and light way, there's more work to do. Avoiding family members is only prolonging the pain and is not a solution. The person still causes the emotional energy to be charged in you and judging them as wrong doesn't solve anything. Work on the energy in solitude and continue to do your personal work until no aversion exists within or in your presence. Our family members are our richest and most needed opportunities for healing. Take advantage of these opportunities to bring yourself closer to your own soul and truth.

Personal Growth

Your emotional block of work is where your treasure is. Working on refining your emotions makes living so much easier! It is a practice of tending to your emotional garden, making space for yourself regularly to feel and allow the messages in your emotions to emerge.

You will reduce your triggers continually and you will get to know yourself by listening and being eager to understand your history and view it as the angels do - divinely purposed for love.

Your soul is waiting underneath the rubble of your emotions and past memories. You need to clear the channel in order to hear your soul's messages about what you came here for. You came to earth to fulfill your soul's purpose and intention but sometimes humans get distracted here and don't complete their purpose. This is very disheartening to them in their last moments!

When you clear and sort out your emotional history, your life purpose will reveal itself in your life's choices.

All is takes is dedication and quiet time well spent.

Intro Questions Answered

How do I control my emotions? We don't control our emotions. We find a balance with them and they help us live our lives more richly.

How can I use my emotions constructively? Feel them to heal them and use the processes in this book to find new ground within yourself. Then use your new joy to create!

Why do other people ignore or invalidate my emotions? People reflect us back to ourselves. Are you ignoring or invalidating your emotions? Teach them how to value your emotions by valuing them yourself.

How can I hide my emotions? If you are upset, you may have to leave the space if you want to cry in private. Hiding them from yourself is impossible. Your emotions want your attention! They have messages for you.

How can I understand and 'deal with' myself? Practice making space to hear your feelings and respect yourself.

Will I outgrow my emotions as I get older? Emotions may reduce somewhat in intensity. But their messages remain until you collect them'

How can I save my emotions for later? Take some deep breaths and tell yourself, you'll listen to your feelings in a more suitable place and time.

How do I understand and work with other people's emotions? Teach others what this book has taught you. Emotions cannot be ignored. They must be allowed to deliver their messages. Emotional well-being is a valuable personal journey.

How can I switch my emotions on and off? You don't want to switch them on and off because you want to be authentic. Feelings are a part of your whole self. Find time to get to know them and your appreciation for your emotions will grow. Then, they will operate very smoothly and richly in your life.

In conclusion, we rise above our emotions by merging with them, learning their wisdom and soaring into higher feeling emotions such as joy and enthusiasm more often then sadness or pain. We have to sweep the floor of the past to make room for the dancing of the future. Your emotions are your friends, and when you take their hands, they will lift you higher than you ever thought you could go!

This book was created to fill a need for those who desire to understand and receive the benefits of cultivating a healthy emotional self. Thank you for reading.

Find more information at
www.cassandraleawilson.com

www.ingramcontent.com/pod-product-compliance
Lightning Source LLC
Chambersburg PA
CBHW032116040426
42449CB00007B/1248